Month-by-Month Poetry
September, October & November

Compiled by Marian Reiner

SCHOLASTIC
PROFESSIONAL **B**OOKS

NEW YORK • TORONTO • LONDON • AUCKLAND • SYDNEY
MEXICO CITY • NEW DELHI • HONG KONG

For Richard, wonderful in all seasons

Cover design by Jaime Lucero
Cover illustration by Amanda Haley
Interior design by Solutions by Design, Inc.
Interior illustration James Graham Hale

ISBN: 0-590-37898-8

Contents

November

Introduction

Welcome to *Month-by-Month Poetry: September, October & November*. This seasonal collection contains more than 60 poems to inspire your students, build literacy, and add sparkle to each day.

Like music, poetry rouses the senses. It causes students to feel deeply and offers comfort, humor, and familiarity. Poetry celebrates! Holidays come alive and ordinary events gain importance when wrapped in the words of a poem. Poetry reinforces the subjects you teach—with rhythm, movement, and rhyme. It builds oral literacy and makes children eager to read. What a wonderful choice you make when you invite poetry into your classroom!

Reach for Poetry

Teachers reach for poetry
And lessons come alive,
Illuminating history
And how to count to five.
Describing common feelings
Or sharing silly tales,
Identifying elephants,
Exploring ants and whales.
No matter what the topic,
How stately or absurd,
When teachers reach for poetry,
They know they will be heard.

—Kathleen M. Hollenbeck

This book is filled with fun, easy-to-read poems to help your students explore fall happenings—from the first day of school through Thanksgiving. You'll find poems about early school jitters, apples, loose teeth, weather changes, making new friends, and more. For easy reference, we've divided the poems by month. September poems relate to the start of school, school tools, and birthdays. October poems explore leaves, apples, and Halloween. Poems for November focus on Thanksgiving, weather, and preparation for winter.

At the beginning of the book, you'll find lots of ideas for using these poems in your classroom. Apply them across the curriculum, and remember: Poetry is enchantment. To build a love for it in your students, you must sprinkle them with poetry. Try not to dissect it or simply repeat it. Work with poetry, play with poetry, read it aloud, and above all, *enjoy it*. Your students will follow your lead.

Activities Ideas

MAKE A BIG BOOK

Use a poem to make your own classroom big book! You might select a poem that explores a highlight of child-hood, such as "Wiggly Tooth," "My Loose Tooth," "Hurray Day!" or "First Day of School." Using an entire sheet of chart paper, write the title of the poem. Then flip to the next piece of chart paper, and write the first line of the poem. Continue in this manner until each line of the poem has its own page. Next, divide the class into small groups. Give each group one page of the story to illustrate. Compile the pages, and staple them together as a book. Seal the binding by covering the staples with wide packing tape or duct tape. Then read your big book aloud!

PUT POEMS IN A POCKET CHART

Write each line of a poem on a separate strip of tagboard. Place the lines in order in the pocket chart, and read the poem aloud. Then use the poem in different ways:

- **Make a rebus.** Cut short strips of tagboard to cover one word in each line of the poem. Select a student to draw a picture on a short strip to represent each word. (For example, draw a squirrel for the word "squirrel.") Have students place the pictures over the appropriate words. Then have them read the poem aloud as a rebus. Poems that work especially well with this are "Painting a Picture" and "Thanksgiving Time."

- **Illustrate the Poem.** Invite your students to draw and cut out characters or objects mentioned in the poem, such as a balloon, a piece of pie, and a slice of pizza for "The Shape of Things." Have students place each picture near its name on the pocket chart.

- **Make a poem puzzle.** Once students are familiar with the poem, remove it from the pocket chart. Mix up the lines, and distribute them. Invite students to read their lines aloud. Then have the class put the poem back in order on the pocket chart.

● **Move to the poem.** Have your class move as the poem indicates, spinning hands round and round to "The Wheels of the Bus" or shaking, running, and scooping to "Autumn Leaves." "The Leaves" is another excellent choice for movement activities.

USE POEMS TO INSPIRE ARTWORK

What better way to illustrate "The Leaves Are Green" than to make leaf prints? On white or colored paper, have students draw a bare tree with brown crayon. Then let them paint real leaves with green tempera, and press these gently around the tree. Or use yellow, red, and orange paint on black paper to illustrate "The Leaves" and "Autumn Leaves."

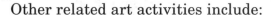

Other related art activities include:

● **Paint what you read.** Read the poem aloud and ask students to paint the same picture the poet describes in "Painting a Picture." Be sure they wiggle the paintbrush to make the worm squirm!

● **Assign colors.** Rewrite the poem "Color" by illustration. Let students answer the poet's questions by drawing or painting their own examples of what is pink, what is red, and so on.

EXPLORE HEALTH AND NUTRITION

Use the poem "Lunch Box, Lunch Box" as a springboard to a discussion of foods that are and are not healthful. Give each student a large piece of construction paper folded in half horizontally. Have students open the paper and lay it flat. On the left side of the fold, have students draw or cut and paste the food items described in the poem (peanut butter sandwich, celery, carrots, banana, and apple). On the right side of the lunchbox, have students draw or cut and paste the foods they brought for lunch that day or foods they would choose in an ideal lunch.

COUNT ON POEMS

Reinforce basic math skills with counting-related poems. For example, based on "Apples Three," you might ask students to glue three paper apples onto a separate piece of paper to create a math sum such as 2 + 1 = 3. They might also draw a picture of the scenario described in "New Friends," in which the subject met three new friends at school. (Ask students to write a corresponding math sum at the bottom of their drawings.) They can also hone counting skills and tune into content by tallying the number of costumes described in the Halloween poem "Spooks."

SEARCH FOR SHAPES

Search for shapes in the classroom after reading "The Shape of Things." Review the shapes discussed in the poem, and have students list other objects of the same shape. Make a graph to record their findings. Your graph might look like this:

SHAPE	ITEMS IN POEM	ITEMS WE FIND
circle	quarter, wheel, moon, bottle cap, big balloon	button, clock, rim of a cup, ear muffs
square	checker board, slice of cheese, TV screen, napkin	desk top, computer screen, counting blocks
rectangle	door, dollar bill, loaf of bread, mattress	math book, chalkboard, window, flag

REINFORCE ABC'S

Depending on the number of students in your class, ask each child to illustrate one or two lines of the poem "Animals From A to Z." Combine their drawings to make an alphabet book for the classroom. Photocopy the book for students to take home and review.

WRITE EXCITING STORIES

Spark creative writing based on poems with exciting themes. Read a poem aloud, and allow students to review it themselves to ponder its plot and meaning. Then ask them to write and/or illustrate their own stories about the poem, sticking to the plot or branching out on their own. Poems that lend themselves well to exciting plots and pictures include "The Leaves," "Pumpkin Surprise," "Halloween Wind," and "Time To Play."

STUDY ANIMAL LIFE

Use poems as a springboard for animal study. Help your students make animal shape books by cutting several pieces of paper in the shape of an animal, stapling the pages together, and writing in facts about the animal. Students might also conduct research to learn more about a specific animal named in a poem and then write their own poems with the details they've learned. Some of the poems that name or tell about animals are "Spider," "Bats," "Squirrels," "Good-bye Geese," "The Animal Song," and "Crow Wonders."

EXPLORE POETRY

Focus on unconventional forms of poetry. Use "When I Walk in the Wind With You" as an example, and invite students to write their own poems that imitate Patricia Hubbell's style.

CELEBRATE THE SEASON

What better time to say "thank you" than at Thanksgiving? Encourage your students to mimic the theme of the poem "Thanksgiving" and make a thank-you placemat to present to a parent or other loved one on the holiday. Provide construction paper for the placemat, with edges trimmed in scallops (optional). Have students draw on the placemat and write/dictate expressions of thanks.

For another dimension of Thanksgiving, display the poem "The Little Girl and the Turkey" on a bulletin board or wall in your classroom. Ask each student to trace his/her outstretched hand on a piece of colored paper to represent a turkey with five feathers. In each "feather," have students write or dictate one thing for which they are thankful. Post these around the poem for a festive display that really does give thanks!

HURRAH FOR HOLIDAYS!

Acknowledge the holidays with light, appealing poems that help students understand and experience the season. "A Halloween Pumpkin," "Little Jack Pumpkin Face," "Pumpkin Surprise," "Thanksgiving Time," and "Turkey Time" are some of the holiday poems featured in this book. Help students recite the poems, clap and tap their rhythm, and imitate their rhyme by writing poems of their own. Encourage students to take lines from a poem and use them as captions for the holiday pictures they draw.

Leavetaking

Vacation is over;
It's time to depart.
I must leave behind
(although it breaks my heart)

Tadpoles in the pond,
A can of eels,
A leaky rowboat,
Abandoned car wheels;

For I'm packing only
Necessities:
A month of sunsets
And two apple trees.

Eve Merriam

September

September is a lady
In a russet gown;
She marches through the country;
She marches through the town;
She stops at every schoolhouse
And rings a magic bell;

She dances on each doorstep
And weaves a magic spell.
She weaves a magic spell that goes
Winging through the land
And gathers children back to school
In a joyous band.

Solveig Paulson Russell

Month-by-Month Poetry: September, October, November   Scholastic Professional Books, 1999

Hurray Day!

Today is the day!
Hurray! Hurray!
It's the first day of school
And *I'm* on my way!

Everything's different!
Nothing's the same!
Because *I'm* going to learn
To write my name!

Patricia Hubbell

First Day of School

I wonder
if my drawing
will be as good as theirs.

I wonder
if they'll like me
or just be full of stares.

I wonder
if my teacher
will look like Mom or Gram.

I wonder
if my puppy
will wonder
where I am.

Aileen Fisher

New Friends

This morning, when
I started school,
I met a girl
named Betty Lou
and she met me—
That made us *two*.

Then, both of us
met Anne Marie—
And that made *three*.

Then, Paul came running
through the door—
Now, the three of us
are *four*—
And I can't wait to meet some more!

Patricia Hubbell

Friendship

A friend is a person who wishes you well,
And keeps all the secrets that you like to tell.

Friends share their toys and their storybooks, too,
Friends can be older or younger than you.

Friends can be real or made up in your mind,
But they're always thoughtful and always kind.

Friends can live nearby or very, very far,
But your friends are your friends, wherever you are!

Risa Jordan

Manners

We say "Thank you."
We say, "Please,"
And "Excuse me," when
When we sneeze.

That's the way
we do what's right.
We have manners.
We're polite.

Helen H. Moore

Writing on the Chalkboard

Up and down my chalk goes.
Squeak, squeak, squeak!
　　Hush, chalk.
　　Don't squawk.
Talk softly when you speak.

Isabel Joshlin Glaser

The Wheels on the Bus

The wheels on the bus go round and round,
Round and round, round and round.
The wheels on the bus go round and round,
All through the town.

The driver on the bus says "Step to the rear!"
"Step to the rear! Step to the rear!"
The driver on the bus says "Step to the rear!"
All through the town.

The people on the bus go up and down
Up and down, up and down.
The people on the bus go up and down
All through the town.

The kids on the bus go yakkity-yak,
Yakkity-yak, yakkity-yak.
The kids on the bus go yakkity-yak,
All through the town.

The driver on the bus says, "Quiet, please!"
"Quiet, please! Quiet, please!"
The driver on the bus says, "Quiet, please!"
All through the town.

The wheels on the bus go round and round,
Round and round, round and round.
The wheels on the bus go round and round.
All through the town.

Anonymous

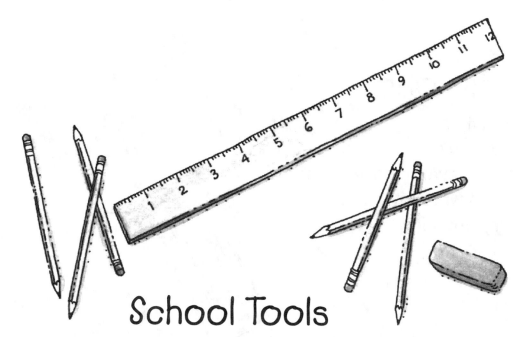

School Tools

I like the look
of my new clean book,
of my pencils six
like pick-up sticks.

I like my eraser
smelling of pink,
wiping mistakes
and helping me think.

I like my ruler
straight as a line
and scissors that cut
paper so fine.

But I like my lunchbox
best of all,
walking to school
in the crisp, new Fall.

Monica Kulling

Pencil Poem

My pencil box
is filled with different colors
like buds flowering from a stem
and I can write my name
in every one of them.

Julia Fields

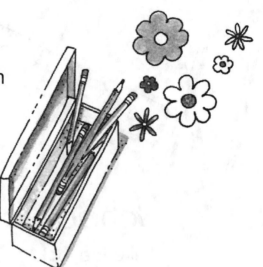

Lunch Box, Lunch Box

Lunch box, lunch box,
what's for lunch?
Peanut butter sandwich
and celery to crunch,
carrots and banana
and an apple to munch.
A bite and a bite
and a *bite* and a BITE,
now I'm heavy
and my lunch box is light.

Eve Merriam

Scissors

A stork with round eyes
opens his shiny, long beak
to cut out paper clouds.

Sandra Liatsos

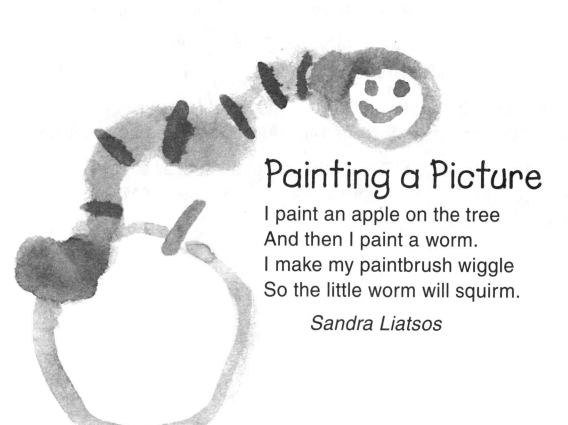

Painting a Picture

I paint an apple on the tree
And then I paint a worm.
I make my paintbrush wiggle
So the little worm will squirm.

Sandra Liatsos

Celebrating Me

I am the only ME I AM who qualifies as me;
no ME I AM has been before, and none will ever be.

No other ME I AM can feel the feelings I've within;
no other ME I AM can fit precisely in my skin.

There is no other ME I AM who thinks the thoughts I do;
the world contains one ME I AM, there is no room for two.

I am the only ME I AM this earth shall ever see;
that ME I AM I always am is no one else but ME!

Anonymous

Feelings

My feelings are funny—
And full of surprise.
Inside my tummy
They're butterflies.

They can turn me red
In my cheeks and ears,
Or ooze from my eyes
In salty tears.

They can make my arms
Go all goose-bumpy.
In my feet
They're happy-jumpy!

Dee Lillegard

Birthday Poem

Happy birthday to you!
Squashed tomatoes and stew;
Eggs and bacon for breakfast,
Happy birthday to you!

Anonymous

Something About Me

There's something about me
That I'm knowing.
There's something about me
That isn't showing.

I'm growing!

Anonymous

A Special Day

Today the sky
is bluer than ever.
Today the birds
will sing forever.
Today I'll shout
and blow my horn.
Today is the day
that I was born!

Sandra Liatsos

Month-by-Month Poetry: September, October, November Scholastic Professional Books, 1999

Birthday Wish

And after they have sung the song,
     the birthday song,
     the song I know,
The candles sparkle on the cake
And then I get to blow
      and blow—

I stand up
And I take a breath
And blow my way
Around the cake

And all my head is dancing with
The birthday wish I get to make!

Myra Cohn Livingston

Birthday Song

At last comes a morning
when nothing is wrong—
When nothing is ragged,
or tattered, or torn—
A lollipop morning
all slick with sweet licks,
When clouds swim in rivers,
bugs balance on sticks,
And even the turtles
attempt some high kicks—
It's my birth happy morning,
My happy birth day,
My Hello-to-the-World,
My Happy Hooray!

Patricia Hubbell

Month-by-Month Poetry: September, October, November Scholastic Professional Books, 1999

My Loose Tooth

I had a loose tooth, a wiggly, jiggly loose tooth.
I had a loose tooth, hanging by a thread.

So I pulled my loose tooth, this wiggly, jiggly loose tooth.
And put it 'neath the pillow when I went up to bed.

The fairies took my loose tooth, my wiggly, jiggly loose tooth.
So now I have a nickel and a hole in my head.

Ruth Kanarek

Wiggly Tooth

Once I had a little tooth
That wobbled every day;
When I ate and when I talked,
It wiggled every way.

Then I had some candy—
A sticky taffy roll;
Now where my wiggly tooth was—
Is nothing but a hole!

Lillie D. Chaffin

Rags

The night wind
rips a cloud sheet
into rags,

then rubs, rubs
the October moon
until it shines
like a brass doorknob.

Judith Thurman

Autumn

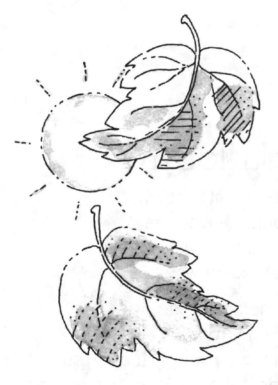

All summer long,
trees studied the sun
to learn the secret
of her fire.

First, they practiced
tracing sunset rays
along their ribs
in colors remembered
from hot summer days.

Now, their chance
on center stage—
they rage yellow gold red,
setting the hills ablaze.

Kristine O'Connell George

Animals From A to Z

A is Ape, B is Bee,
C is Clownfish in the sea!

D is Deer, E is Eel,
F's a Fox who wants a meal.

G is Goose, H is Hog,
I's an Inchworm on a log.

Jay is J, Koala's K,
L's a Lion far away.

M is Mule, N is Newt,
O's an Ostrich tall and cute.

P is Pig, Q is Quail,
R's a Rat with curly tail.

Snake is S, Turkey's T,
U's the Umbrella bird flying free.

V is Viper, Worm is W,
Bird's X are hatching. (Does that joke trouble you?)

Yak is Y, Zebra's Z,
Alphabet animals for you and me!

Meish Goldish

The Animal Song

Alligator, hedgehog, anteater, bear,
Rattlesnake, buffalo, anaconda, hare.

Bullfrog, woodchuck, wolverine, goose,
Whippoorwill, chipmunk, jackal, moose.

Mud turtle, whale, glowworm, bat,
Salamander, snail, and Maltese cat.

Polecat, dog, wild otter, rat,
Pelican, hog, dodo, and bat.

House rat, toe rat, white deer, doe,
Chickadee, peacock, bobolink, and crow.

Anonymous

Month-by-Month Poetry: September, October, November   Scholastic Professional Books, 1999

Color

What is pink? A rose is pink
By a fountain's brink.

What is red? A poppy's red
In its barley bed.

What is blue? The sky is blue
Where the clouds float through.

What is white? A swan is white
Sailing in the light.

What is yellow? Pears are yellow,
Rich and ripe and mellow.

What is green? The grass is green,
With small flowers between.

What is violet? Clouds are violet
In the summer twilight.

What is orange? Why, an orange,
Just an orange!

Christina Rossetti

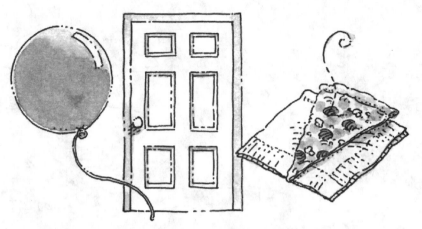

The Shape of Things

What is a circle? What is round?
A quarter rolling on the ground.
A wheel is a circle, so is the moon,
A bottle cap, or a big balloon.

What is a square, with sides the same?
The wooden board for a checker game.
A slice of cheese, a TV screen,
A table napkin to keep you clean.

What is a rectangle, straight or tall?
The door that stands within your wall.
A dollar bill, a loaf of bread,
The mattress lying on your bed.

What is a triangle, with sides of three?
A piece of pie for you and me.
A musical triangle, ding, ding, ding,
A slice of pizza with everything!

These are the shapes seen everywhere:
A triangle, rectangle, circle, square.
If you look closely where you've been,
You'll surely see the shapes you're in!

Meish Goldish

Days of the Week

(sung to "Sing a Song of Sixpence")

Sing a song of Monday,
Helping to shop.
Sing a song of Tuesday,
Popcorn to pop.
Sing a song of Wednesday,
Books to begin.
Sing a song of Thursday,
When I play the violin!

Sing a song of Friday,
Riding my bike.
Sing a song of Saturday,
Taking a hike.
Sing a song of Sunday,
Out playing ball.
Every day of every week's
My favorite day of all!

Meish Goldish

A New World

Columbus found a new world
    Because he dared to do
A thing that was unheard of—
    A thing that was quite new.

Columbus found a new world
    Because he made a start,
Instead of merely pond'ring o'er
    The thoughts within his heart.

Columbus found a new world
    Because he saw things through—
And you can find your new world
    Precisely that way, too.

Alice Crowell Hoffman

Apple Song

The apples are seasoned
And ripe and sound.
Gently they fall
On the yellow ground.

The apples are stored
In the dusky bin
Where hardly a glimmer
Of light creeps in.

In the firelit, winter
Nights, they'll be
The clear sweet taste
Of a summer tree!

Frances Frost

Apples Three

fresh picked apples
from an apple tree
one for you
and one for me
one for teacher
that makes three
apples picked
from an apple tree

Monica Kulling

If You Were Here, Johnny Appleseed

If you were here,
Johnny Appleseed,
you would see all
the beautiful trees
full of apples
shining down the long,
long fields.
You would feel
proud that you hiked
those many hard miles
to plant apple seeds.

If you were here,
you would eat
the warm apple pie,
taste the applesauce.
You would tell me
that in those days
when your feet grew
tired and more tired,
you could still see
in your mind's eye
the apple trees you knew
would grow.

Sandra Liatsos

Crow Wonders

Crow knows
that hat,
that baggy coat,
that raggy ruff at the throat—
Old stuff!

The straw man
hasn't fluttered
a hand,
muttered a sound,
and the corn is sweet.

But what's
that dark thing
at his feet,
growing longer
longer
in
the
sun?

Lilian Moore

The Leaves

The leaves had a wonderful frolic.
  They danced to the wind's loud song.
They whirled, and they floated, and scampered.
  They circled and flew along.

The moon saw the little leaves dancing.
  Each looked like a small brown bird.
The man in the moon smiled and listened,
  And this is the song he heard.

The North Wind is calling, is calling,
  And we must whirl round and round,
And then, when our dancing is ended,
  We'll make a warm quilt for the ground.

Anonymous

The Leaves Are Green

The leaves are green, the nuts are brown,
They hang so high they won't come down.
Leave them alone till frosty weather,
Then they will all come down together.

Old Rhyme

Month-by-Month Poetry: September, October, November Scholastic Professional Books, 1999

Autumn Leaves

Down
      down
            down
Red
      yellow
            brown
Autumn leaves tumble down,
Autumn leaves crumble down,
Autumn leaves bumble down,
Flaking and shaking,
Tumbledown leaves.

Skittery
Flittery
Rustle by
Hustle by
Crackle and crunch
In a snappety bunch.

Run and catch
Run and catch
Butterfly leaves
Sailboat leaves
Windstorm leaves.
Can you catch them?

Swoop,
Scoop,
Pile them up
In a stompy pile and
Jump
      Jump
      JUMP!

Eve Merriam

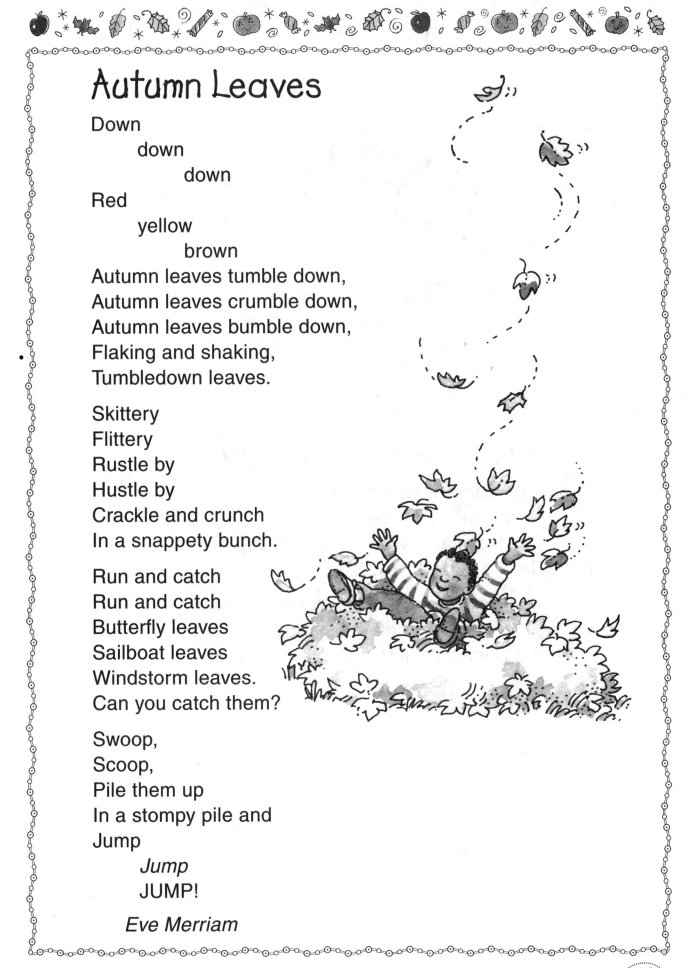

Month-by-Month Poetry: September, October, November Scholastic Professional Books, 1999

A Halloween Pumpkin

They chose me from my brother: "That's the
Nicest one," they said,
And they carved me out a face and put a
Candle in my head;

And they set me on the doorstep. Oh, the
Night was dark and wild;
But when they lit the candle, then I
Smiled!

Dorothy Aldis

Little Jack Pumpkin Face

Little Jack Pumpkin Face
    Lived on a vine,
Little Jack Pumpkin Face
    Thought it was fine.

First he was small and green,
    Then big and yellow,
Little Jack Pumpkin Face
    Is a fine fellow.

Country Song

Pumpkin Surprise

I was choosing a pumpkin,
A fat orange pumpkin,
When I spotted a hole
In its side—
A hole like a door,
A little round door,
A door that led straight
To a house—
In the space of a minute
I saw what was in it,
—*It wasn't a thing you'd forget!*
Curled in that pumpkin,
That fat orange pumpkin,
Was a fat little, gray little MOUSE.
A mouse in a house in a pumpkin!
On a floor that was covered with seeds,
Curled up and cozy,
Snoozy and dozy,
Asleep on a soft bed of weeds!

Patricia Hubbell

Halloween Wind

The wind came trick-or-treating
down our quiet street.
It rattled all the windows
and then we heard it beat
on every door at every house
where shutters banged and
clattered.
It howled for treats and howled
for more
while leaves and branches
scattered.
It rolled a pumpkin down the
street,
and made the cat's fur rise.
Then after all the tricks it played
it flew up in the sky
with candy wrappers in its grasp,
and empty bags and sticks—
It hadn't wanted treats at all,
only lots of tricks!

Sandra Liatsos

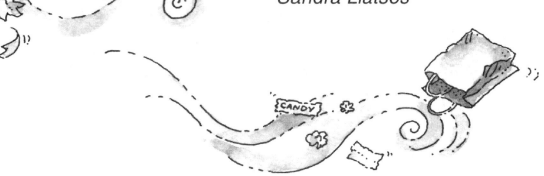

Skeleton

Tink, plonk, konkle;
Midnight
Wind-chime;
Clinking, clanking, dancing
To the
Tonkle, plink, konk
Of its
Own
Hollow,
Dangling
Bones.

Lee Bartlett

Spooks

There's a goblin at my window,
A monster by my door.
The pumpkin at my table
Keeps on smiling more and more.
There's a ghost who haunts my
bedroom,
A witch whose face is green.
They used to be my family,
Till they dressed for Halloween.

Sandra Liatsos

Bats

When the sun goes down,
Bats wake from their sleep.
They begin to stir
And squeak and peep.

Then they dart about
Their cavernous room,
Anxious for
The deepening gloom.

They pour from their cave
Out into the night,
Huge black clouds
In hungry flight.

Gobbling beetles
And moths as they fly,
They darken the already
Darkened sky . . .

Only returning
When night grows gray
To hang from their ceilings
And sleep all day.

Dee Lilligard

Spider

Spider's
spinning

Spider's
beginning

another web.

(Spin
low)

Thinning her long
and silky
thread

(Spin
high)

Spider's
spinning
her
silver lace.

Isn't her web
a lovely
place?

Ask fly.

Lilian Moore

Thumping, Stumping, Bumping, Jumping

Thumping, stumping, bumping, jumping,
Ripping, nipping, tripping, skipping,
All the way home.

Popping, clopping, stopping, hopping,
Stalking, chalking, talking, walking,
All the way home.

Anonymous

Squirrels

Some little red squirrels
Live up in a tree,
Out in the woodland gay.
They frisk and frolic,
And scamper about,
On each bright autumn day.

But they are not idle;
They're working away,
Busy as they can be,
Filling a storehouse,
For long winter days,
Thrifty and wise, you see.

Winifred C. Marshall

Whisky Frisky

Whisky frisky,
Hipperty hop,
Up he goes
To the tree top!

Whirly, twirly,
Round and round,
Down he scampers
To the ground.

Furly, curly,
What a tail,
Tall as a feather,
Broad as a sail.

Where's his supper?
In the shell.
Snappy, cracky,
Out it fell.

Anonymous

The Owl and the Wind

Oh, did you hear the wind last night
 A-blowing right at you?
It sounded just as though it said,
 "Oooo—ooo—oooo!"

The wind now has a playmate,
 Just as most children do,
He sits up in a tree and hoots,
 "To-whoo, to-whit, to-whoo."

So when you hear the owl and wind
 Just at the close of day,
They're calling to each other
 To come out now and play.

Madeline A. Chaffee

Month-by-Month Poetry: September, October, November Scholastic Professional Books, 1999

Time to Play

A rabbit said to Mr. Squirrel,
    One chilly autumn day,
"I think you are quite foolish
    To hide those nuts away."

"Oho! my friend," said Mr. Squirrel,
    "The cold winds soon will blow,
And nuts will all be hidden
    Deep under drifts of snow.

"Now that is why I'm working
    With all my strength today;
When winter comes, I'll doubtless
    Have time enough for play."

Ada Clark

Fly South Geese

Fly south geese go—soon
    the earth will be covered in
        ice and snow—it's time
            to leave for warmer winds so
                go— before winter begins.

Linda Kulp

Mid-November

After a long silence,
a few birds sing;
they're back,
blue jay and cardinal,
singing along with hardheaded leaves
that hang on high branches
and crick-crack the wind—
singing as my sister and I,
half-drowned in red and yellow
leaves, join them with our song.

Emanuel di Pasquale

Month-by-Month Poetry: September, October, November Scholastic Professional Books, 1999

When I Walk in the Wind With You

When
I
Walk
In the
Wind
With
You
Our
Scarves
Are
Birds
Flying
Together

Patricia Hubbell

First Book

Hey everybody,
Come look, come look –

I'm reading, I'm reading,
I'm reading a book!

I just found it right here
On the library shelf
And I can read every word
All by myself—

Hey everybody,
come look, come look

I'm reading—
I'm reading—
My very first book!

Linda Kulp

Bookworm

A bookworm of curious breed
Took a bite of a book out of greed
　　When he found it was tasty,
　　He said, "I've been hasty.
I think I shall learn how to read."

Mary Ann Hoberman

Easy to Open

Easy to open,
No need to unlock it.
Sometimes it's small enough
To carry in your pocket.
But when it is open
It can carry *you*
Through fascinating spaces
Like a far-flying rocket.

Question: What is it?
Answer: A book

Lillian Morrison

We Could Be Friends

We could be friends
Like friends are supposed to be.
You, picking up the telephone
Calling me

 to come over and play
 or take a walk,
 finding a place
 to sit and talk,

Or just goof around
Like friends do,
Me, picking up the telephone
Calling you.

Myra Cohn Livingston

What's Your Name?

What's your name?
Mary Jane.
Where do you live?
Down the lane.
What do you keep?
A little shop.
What do you sell?
Ginger pop.
How many bottles do you sell
    in a day?
Twenty-four, now go away.

Traditional

Jump Rope Rhyme

Can you keep a secret?
I don't suppose you can.
You mustn't laugh or giggle
While I tickle your hand.

Anonymous

Lily Lee

I like Lily,
Little Lily Lee;
I like Lily
And Lily likes me.
Lily likes lollipops,
Lemonade and lime-drops,
But I like Lily,
Little Lily Lee.

Isobel Best

The Pilgrims Came

The Pilgrims came across the sea,
And never thought of you and me;
And yet it's very strange the way
We think of them Thanksgiving Day.

We tell their story old and true
Of how they sailed across the blue,
And found a new land to be free
And built their homes quite near the sea.

The people think that they were sad,
And grave; I'm sure that they were glad—
They made Thanksgiving Day—that's fun—
We thank the Pilgrims every one!

Annette Wynne

Thanksgiving Time

When all the leaves are off the boughs,
  And nuts and apples gathered in,
And cornstalks waiting for the cows,
  And pumpkins safe in barn and bin:

Then mother says: "My children dear,
  The fields are brown and autumn flies;
Thanksgiving Day is very near,
  And we must make Thanksgiving pies!"

Country Rhyme

Turkey Time

Thanksgiving Day will soon by here;
It comes around but once a year.
If I could only have my way,
We'd have Thanksgiving every day!

Anonymous

The Little Girl and the Turkey

The little girl said
As she asked for more:
"But what is the Turkey
Thankful for?"

Dorothy Aldis

Thanksgiving

Thank You

    for all my hands can hold—

        apples red,

           and melons gold,

             yellow corn

                both ripe and sweet,

                  peas and beans

                    so good to eat!

Thank You

    for all my eyes can see—

        lovely sunlight,

           field and tree,

             white cloud-boats

                in sea-deep sky,

                  soaring bird

                    and butterfly.

Thank You

    for all my ears can hear—

        birds' song echoing

           far and near,

             songs of little

                stream, big sea,

                  cricket, bullfrog,

                    duck and bee!

Ivy O. Eastwick

Month-by-Month Poetry: September, October, November   Scholastic Professional Books, 1999